The Right Kite

By Cameron Macintosh

Dad and Cass went to get
a kite from Mike's shop.

"What is the best kite
for me?" said Cass.

"I think this kite will be right,"
said Mike.

"I will try it!" said Cass.

Dad and Cass went
to try the kite.

Cass ran with the kite.

t went up ...

Cass went up a bit, too!

Dad got a big fright.

"We did not like this kite,"
said Dad to Mike.

"It can fly **too** well!"
said Cass.

Yes, you are too light
or that kite," said Mike.
"This kite might be
he right size!"

Cass ran with the kite.

It went high in the sky.

But if Cass did not run,
it fell down.

Cass gave a big sigh.

'Let's go back and try
one last kite," said Dad.

"This kite is not quite right
for me," Cass said to Mike.
"Can I try that one this time?"

Yes! That will be the right kite,"
said Mike.

Dad and Cass went back
to the sand.

Cass ran with the kite.

It went high up in the sky!

This is the right kite!"
said Cass.

I'm very glad!" said Dad,
with a big sigh.

CHECKING FOR MEANING

1. Why didn't Cass get the first kite she tried? *(Literal)*

2. What did Cass have to do to stop the second kite from falling down? *(Literal)*

3. How did Cass know the third kite was the right kite for her? *(Inferential)*

EXTENDING VOCABULARY

fright	What is another word that has a similar meaning to *fright*? E.g. scare, shock.
light	What does *light* mean in this story? What is its opposite? Do you know another meaning of the word *light*?
sigh	What is a *sigh*? Why do people sigh? Are they tired, angry or sad?

MOVING BEYOND THE TEXT

1. Talk about a time when you have flown a kite. Where were you? Who was with you?

2. Where are safe places to fly kites? Why?

3. What are kites made from? What colours can they be? What shapes are they?

4. If you went to buy a kite, what type would you choose?

SPELLINGS FOR THE LONG /i/ VOWEL SOUND

i	igh	i_e	y	ie

PRACTICE WORDS

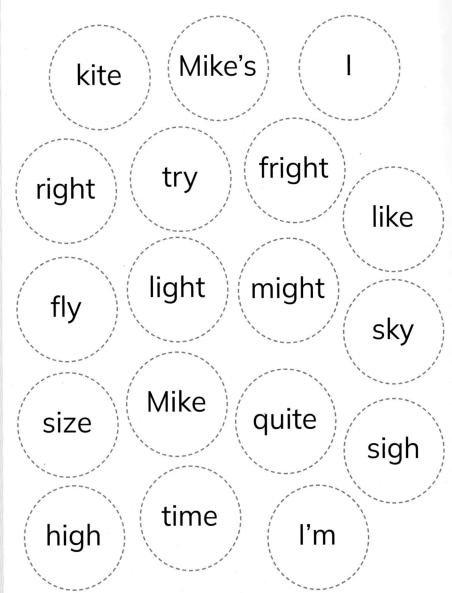

kite

Mike's

I

right

try

fright

like

fly

light

might

sky

size

Mike

quite

sigh

high

time

I'm